THE SOUTH

GALLERY BOOKS
An Imprint of W. H. Smith Publishers Inc.
112 Madison Avenue
New York City 10016

This edition first published in U.S.
in 1990 by Gallery Books,
an imprint of W.H. Smith Publishers, Inc.
112 Madison Avenue, New York, New York 10016

ISBN 0-8317-8835-6

Printed and bound in Spain

For rights information about the photographs in
this book please contact:

The Image Bank
111 Fifth Avenue, New York, NY 10003

Producer: Solomon M. Skolnick
Author: Moira Duggan
Design Concept: Leslie Ehlers
Designer: Ann-Louise Lipman
Editor: Madelyn Larsen
Production: Valerie Zars
Photo Researcher: Edward Douglas
Assistant Photo Researcher: Robert Hale

Title page: *Statue of Captain John
Smith at Jamestown, Virginia.*
Opposite: *Replicas of English
sailing ships.*

The South is border states, Deep South states, and eastern seaboard states. It's an area with a reputation for hospitality and charm, but the best way then to get a feel for its vastness and scope is to look at each of the individual states that make up the South.

VIRGINIA is a panorama of colonial and Civil War history. But what stirs the pride of Virginians is the state's extraordinary role in the founding of the nation. The first permanent English settlement in America was Jamestown, founded in 1607 at the mouth of the James River. Jamestown settlement, a National Historical Park, is a re-creation of the original village, including replicas of the ships that brought the settlers from England. Progress during the first hundred years of settlement may be judged by a visit to Colonial Williamsburg, a restoration of the town founded as a seat of government in 1699. Its Capitol, Governor's Palace, and College of William and Mary, brick buildings of Georgian design, are a world apart from the log palisades of early Jamestown.

Opposite: *Beyond the marsh grass, replicas of the three ships that brought the first settlers to Virginia.* This page: *Scenes from Colonial Williamsburg: Governor's Palace, interior of the "Powder Horn," or Public Magazine' shop of the instrument makers; octagonal Magazine, with walls 8 feet thick.*

Mount Vernon, plantation home of George Washington, overlooking the Potomac River near Alexandria, Virginia. Monticello, Thomas Jefferson's house near Charlottesville, Virginia, built to his own design; the dome was most unusual for its time.

Two powerful traditions—representative government and the family as an institution—helped make Virginia a breeding ground for leaders. Indeed, of the first twelve Presidents of the United States, seven were Virginians.

George Washington lived almost half a century at the house and plantation he called Mount Vernon. The house, with many of its original furnishings, gives an intimate glimpse into the mind and times of the man who was called "first in the hearts of his countrymen."

Thomas Jefferson's house, Monticello, stands on a mountaintop near Charlottesville. Immaculately restored, it is endlessly fascinating, for Jefferson was statesman, philosopher, architect, inventor, and gentleman farmer.

Top to bottom: *Stratford, built in the shape of an H, was the ancestral home of Confederate General Robert E. Lee. Carlyle House in Alexandria, a Georgian Colonial mansion completed in 1753. Shop fronts in Alexandria's historic Old Town.*

A C-shaped curve, beginning in Alexandria and ending in the Tidewater, takes in much of the grandeur of Virginia. Alexandria, across the Potomac River from Washington, D.C., has a Historic District with brick-paved streets and many charming eighteenth-century houses. Moving west from here, one enters the Blue Ridge Mountains and fox-hunting country, whose vistas and greenery are best seen in springtime from the Skyline Drive, which follows the crest of the Blue Ridge for 105 miles.

West of this range lies the valley of the Shenandoah River, a region of historic towns, fertile farmlands, and people who cherish old ways. From here the road east toward Williamsburg passes several historic plantation houses. This is the Tidewater, where four great rivers empty into the Chesapeake Bay. Enclosing the Bay on the east is a roughly indented peninsula where fishermen live, as they have for many generations, in tiny villages, and wild ponies run on broad Atlantic beaches.

Top to bottom: *Equestrian statue of Confederate General Stonewall Jackson at Manassas National Battlefield Park. At Arlington National Cemetery, a soldier places wreath at Tomb of the Unknowns. Behind it is the columned portico of the Memorial Amphitheater. General Douglas MacArthur Memorial, a four-building complex in Norfolk.* Opposite: *The Confederate Monument, a granite column crowned with a statue of a soldier, is a Norfolk landmark.*

KENTUCKY, which Daniel Boone explored between 1769 and 1771, he brought back news of a "second paradise." Its most remarkable geographic feature, between the mountainous east and the Ohio River Valley that forms its oblique western boundary, is the celebrated Bluegrass Country in the north central part of the state. The breeding of Thoroughbred race horses is a major industry here.

Kentucky has its share of gracious homes built by wealthy farmers and breeders, and perhaps white porticoes are nowhere seen to better advantage than across a vista of green Kentucky meadows. Yet the state is known, too, for a far humbler type of dwelling, the log cabin. A famous example may be seen at the Abraham Lincoln Historic Site about an hour's drive south of Louisville. Here a neoclassical stone temple encloses a tiny log cabin believed to have been the

Above: *The Scope, Norfolk's sports arena, designed by Pier Luigi Nervi and completed in 1972.* Below and opposite: *Rotunda of the Virginia State Capitol, built between 1785 and 1799 to a design by Thomas Jefferson. Building is modeled on a Roman temple.*

Left: *Thoroughbreds at play in Bluegrass meadows of Kentucky.* Below: *Kentucky Derby, first contest in flat racing's Triple Crown, is run each May at historic Churchill Downs track in Louisville.*

birthplace of Lincoln. Also near Louisville is Fort Knox, where a bomb-proof granite building protects treasure of a different sort—the United States' gold bullion reserves. In Louisville itself is Churchill Downs, site of America's premier horse race for three-year-old Thoroughbreds, the Kentucky Derby.

TENNESSEE shares with North Carolina one of the most beautiful parks in the nation, the half-million-acre Great Smoky National Park, named for the blue haze that gives its peaks and valleys a mysterious allure.

Perhaps Tennessee's most famous export is music. Nashville is both the creative and industrial capital of country-and-western music. Not far from Nashville, the Grand Old Opry is the centerpiece of a theme park called Opryland.

Top to bottom: *Fisherman's shacks along a quiet backwater of the Mississippi River. Sidewheelers at their docks along the Mississippi River in Memphis. Grave of Elvis Presley at Graceland, his house in Memphis.*

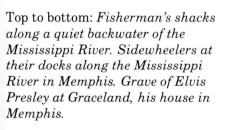

Opposite: *A house in classic plantation style, Graceland welcomes more than half a million visitors each year.* This page: *Wooded Lynchburg, Tennessee, is home of the famous Jack Daniels Distillery, the oldest registered distillery in the United States.* Below: *A taste of the past may be had at old-time Country Store, part of George A. Dickel Distillery near Tullahoma, Tennessee.*

This page and opposite: *Nashville, with its modern skyline, could be called "the city that country music built." A Nashville landmark is this full-scale replica of the Greek Parthenon, one of the reasons the city is called "the Athens of the South." Visitors to Nashville can see the city and its environs from tour boats that ply the Cumberland River. Ionic columns and a round tower distinguish the Tennessee State Capitol (center), designed by William Strickland and completed in 1859.*

Above left to right: *Nighttime vista in Nashville. Axis leads to War Memorial for Tennessee soldiers who died in World War I, seen also in close-up. One of Nashville's newest and handsomest skyscrapers is the Third National Financial Center, completed in 1986.* Below: *Nature adds its own dramatic illumination to Nashville's city lights.* Opposite: *The new and the old are close neighbors in Knoxville. Here the handsome new Riverview Tower reflects the clock tower of the 19th-century Court House.*

This page: *James White Fort is a replica of the first settlers' cabin in the Knoxville area. Riverview Tower and its companion skyscraper, Plaza Tower, soar in the background. Knoxville's sleek, low-rise City County Building is well suited to its riverfront site. Opposite: Near Miller Park in downtown Chattanooga are two notable buildings—the pie-shaped One Central Plaza and the Dome Building, with its graceful domed cupola.*

This page: *The train made famous in the song "Chattanooga Choo-Choo" pulled into this monumental terminal. It is now a shop-and-hotel complex in which railroad cars are used as guest rooms. Portrait of Chattanooga as evening shadows fall. Opposite: Mists lingering in the valleys and hollows give the Great Smoky Mountains their name.*

Preceding pages: *Biltmore House, a French Renaissance-style chateau designed by Richard Morris Hunt and completed in 1895, is the centerpiece of Pisgah National Forest at Asheville, North Carolina. Rising sun adds fiery splendor to the glass-walled skyscrapers of Charlotte, North Carolina.* This page: *The Old Well on the campus of the University of North Carolina at Chapel Hill. "Old East" (background) is the oldest standing state university building in the United States.* Below: *Aerial view of the campus of Duke University, Durham.*

Tennessee's other music capital—yes, there are two—is Memphis, which overlooks the Mississippi River in the extreme southwest corner of this long state. Memphis became the birthplace of the blues when the great blues originator, W.C. Handy, played here on Beale Street. The memory of rock 'n' roll king Elvis Presley is also preserved here: his house, Graceland, where he is buried, draws tens of thousands of reverent and curious visitors yearly.

NORTH CAROLINA has distinctly unique geographical areas. The Outer Banks, especially the Cape Hatteras National Seashore, are superb vacation-lands, not just because of their wide beaches but also for their friendly and dependable inhabitants and excellent seafood. The coastal plain has long provided the state's chief money crop, tobacco, and this in turn became the basis of its immensely important cigarette industry. West of the plain, the land rises to the Piedmont Plateau, where corporations, universities, factories, and farms are making this one of the most prosperous regions in the South.

Top to bottom: *Government buildings in state capital, Raleigh, include Greek Revival Capitol (1840), Edward Durell Stone's pyramid-roofed Legislative Building (1936), and the new, high-rise Archives Building.*

Opposite: *Fayetteville Street Mall in downtown Raleigh.* This page: *At Kill Devil Hills on the Outer Banks of North Carolina, Wright Brothers National Monument marks the spot where the aviation pioneers made their first powered flight. This biplane is one of many exhibits in the interpretive museum.*

Opposite: *Abandoned lighthouse on Cape Hatteras, North Carolina.* This page: *Inundated shoreline at Bull Island, one of South Carolina's barrier islands, where the ceaseless waves constantly refigure the contours of the land.* Right: *Harbour Town village and marina on Hilton Head Island offers luxurious port facilities.*

Above: Scenes from picturesque Charleston, South Carolina. Hexagonal bell tower of St. Michael's Episcopal Church, (1752-61). St. Phillip's Episcopal Church, built of stone in Greek Revival style (1735-38), is remarkable for its landmark multitiered spire. Dock Street Theatre, liberally embellished with ironwork, occupies a structure built as a hotel in 1809. Below: Arched and columned porches of the Calhoun Mansion make the most of shade and cooling breezes.

This page: *This fortress-like building is part of the Military College of South Carolina, better known as The Citadel. Houses, as a rule, are painted white in Charleston, hence the name Rainbow Row for this unusual group on East Bay Street.*

Opposite: *Cypress Gardens, north of Charleston, is a 160-acre preserve where ancient cypresses, flowering plants, and many forms of wildlife live in harmony.* Above: *Tall skyscrapers punctuate the skyline of Atlanta.* Below: *Baseball fans pack Atlanta Stadium as the home team Braves play under the lights.*

Left to right: *A quick tour of Atlanta. Robert Woodruff Arts Center, home of the Atlanta Symphony Orchestra. Phoenix Statue, honoring the city's revival after Union General Sherman's incendiary visit. Jimmy Carter Presidential Center houses the papers of the former President. Swan House, headquarters of The Atlanta Historical Society. Tomb of Dr. Martin Luther King, Jr., a native of Atlanta. The State Capitol (1889), modeled on the National Capitol.* Opposite, top: *Immense carving on Stone Mountain depicts (left to right) Jefferson Davis, Robert E. Lee, and Stonewall Jackson, heroes of the Confederacy.* Below: *Three-dimensional Cyclorama of the Battle of Atlanta is 400 feet in circumference.*

Although North Carolina's institutions of higher learning— Duke University, the University of North Carolina, and North Carolina State University— have helped put the state in the forefront of science and technology, the state is still largely rural. Visitors can enjoy outdoor recreation of all sorts— hiking in the Great Smokies, golfing and horse sports in the central Sandhills area, birdwatching and fishing along the coast.

SOUTH CAROLINA draws many travelers. Business of course, is one reason. Or the visitor might come to experience Charleston, one of the South's most beautiful and interesting cities. In the early days, plantation families retreated to this coastal city in summer for relief from the humidity and mosquitoes of the Low Country. Their standards of comfort and civility are still evident—in the well-maintained houses, the nearest lanes, the carefully planted gardens. Charleston is the host city of the Spoleto Festival USA, almost two weeks of music, dance, theater, and opera presentations.

Probably the greatest number of visitors come to the barrier islands, several of which have been extensively developed as vacation resorts. Hilton Head and Kiawah have the most luxurious facilities, which include championship golf courses and large marinas. Considerable land has been set aside for nature preserves on the barrier islands, and the broad flat beaches beckon to walkers, bike riders, and bathers.

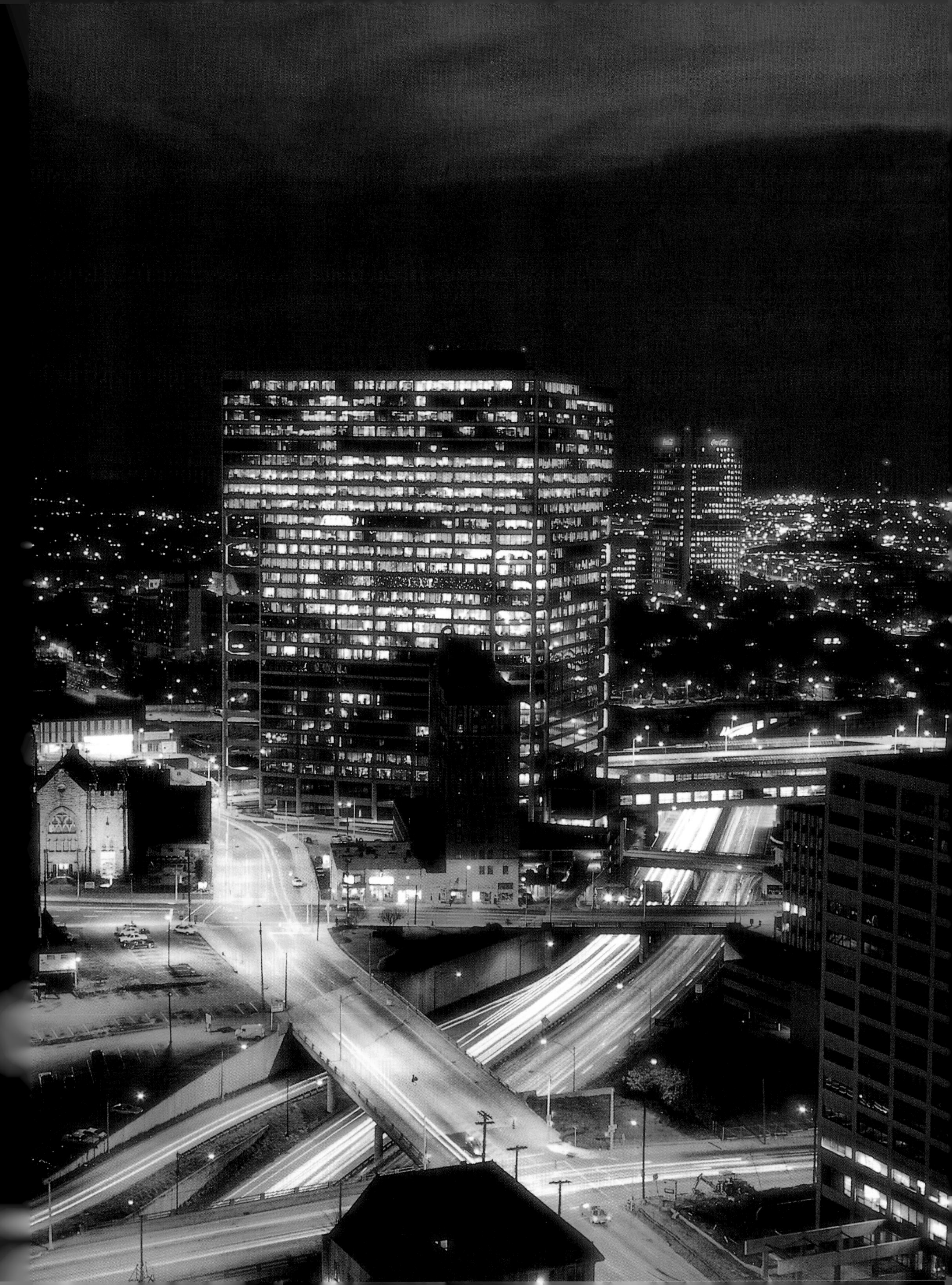

Opposite: *Nighttime view captures the hard-working, fast-moving spirit of Atlanta. On the Georgia coast, the port city of Savannah guards its fine architectural tradition.* This page: *Two of its notable buildings are the Old Cotton Exchange (1887), part of Factors' Row along the wharves, and Christ Episcopal Church (1838), in the Greek Revival style.*

Above: *Plaque on Jekyll Island, Georgia, honors the island's oldest and largest tree. Grace Episcopal Church serves a Sea Island congregation established in 1736 and preached to by John Wesley. On the Georgia coast, Midway church (1792) is a clapboard building of moving simplicity. Below: Pennant flying, castellated Jekyll Island Club, a turn-of-the-century resort for millionaires from the North, is newly renovated.*

Above: *Nighttime portrait of Jacksonville, northeast Florida's most dynamic city.* Below: *Setting sun profiles the fortress walls of Castillo de San Marcos, the oldest building in St. Augustine.*

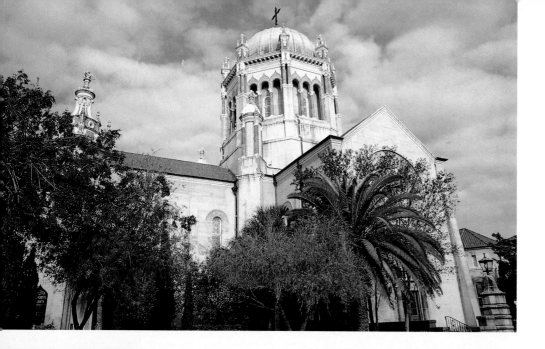

GEORGIA today is a place of remarkable contrasts. It is the low sea islands along its Atlantic shore and the Blue Ridge Mountains in its northwest corner. It is long-established agricultural ways and the urban phenomenon of Atlanta, whose assets include the offices of hundreds of major corporations and several U.S. Government agencies, unparalleled convention facilities, an international airport that is the aviation hub of the Southeast, and a population of energetic people who are eager to make Atlanta "the world's next great city."

Savannah, a key East Coast port, is also a model of architectural preservation, with many residential blocks where Regency-style houses surround tree-planted squares.

An entirely different atmosphere attracts travelers to the coast, where the many barrier islands—St. Simon's, Jekyll, and Cumberland—offer a balance of vacation resorts and preserved coastal environments. Here one can still experience the dialect and cuisine known as Gullah, whose origins are in good part African.

Top to bottom: *Flagler Memorial Presbyterian Church in St. Augustine was built by railroad magnate Henry Flagler in memory of his daughter. Cypress Gardens is a botanical extravaganza covering 223 acres east of Tampa. At Sea World in Orlando killer whales perform precision routines with human partners.*

As a last comment on contrasts, consider the national parks of Georgia: the watery glooms of the vast Okefenokee Swamp in the southeast seem to be a world apart from the mountain ranges of the Chattahoochee National Forest on the northern border, where a 4,780-foot peak called Brasstown Bald stands as the highest point in the state.

FLORIDA, more than other southern states, shows most emphatically the imprint of the twentieth century. The rush to modernity has dramatically changed the face of this low-lying state, whose largest town in 1880 was Key West, with some 10,000 residents.

Most of Florida's famous sites (excluding the celebrated Disney World and Epcot Center) are on or near its long eastern coastline. St. Augustine in the north is the nation's oldest city. Daytona, with its broad beach of firm sand, began attracting auto racers at the turn of the century and now hosts the annual Daytona 500 auto race. At Cape Canaveral is the Kennedy Space Center, where everything seems gargantuan: the 45-story-tall

Above: *Snow White charms visitors to Walt Disney World Magic Kingdom in Orlando.* Right: *Nearby is Disney's theme park, EPCOT Center, with its 180-foot-high geosphere called "Spaceship Earth."*

service gantry, the Vertical basilica, and the crawler-transporter capable of carrying 6,000-ton rockets. At Palm Beach, farther north, society holds sway in an enclave of Spanish-Moorish-style mansions where polo, croquet, and charity galas help the days pass agreeably. Miami, near the southern tip of Florida, started as a beach resort and today is an important and ultramodern business center.

The Everglades, a 5,000-square-mile area of marshes, swamps, mangroves, and sawgrass, make up almost the entire lower third of Florida and include the country's third-largest national park, Everglades NP.

Florida tails off in a series of coral and limestone islands called the Florida Keys, which are connected by a narrow highway more than a hundred miles long. At the end of the road is Key West, whose residents celebrate the carefree life.

Top to bottom: *Visitors return again and again to experience Walt Disney World's happy blend of fantasy, adventure, and nostalgia. Opposite: Rocket display is part of the huge Kennedy Space Center at Cape Canaveral. Boca Raton Hotel and Club, with its Moorish-style fountain, opened as The Cloister Inn in 1926, designed by architect Addison Mizner.*

This page and opposite: *Superbly equipped marinas, like this one at the city's edge, sustain Miamians' passion for boating in all forms. Tourist hotels jostle each other along the strip of sand called Miami Beach. Art Deco architecture and embellishments at Miami Beach are now a tourist attraction in their own right. This famous football arena is the Orange Bowl, home of the University of Miami Hurricanes.*

This page: *Parrot Jungle in Miami is the place to see these exotic birds flying free. Villa Viscaya, a mansion in the Mediterranean style, was built by industrialist James Deering and completed in 1922. No expense was spared in achieving grandeur in the house and formal gardens, which today are open to the public. The stone boat acts as a breakwater.*

Dwarf cypress trees and bird rookery on Florida Bay are two of the many diverse environments in the huge Florida Everglades.

In contrast to the east coast, the Gulf Coast of Florida is irregular, with bays and inlets and offshore islands. The Florida boom has not been so all-consuming here, and many Americans settle in Gulf Coast towns in their retirement years to enjoy placid waters and beaches that are a shell collector's paradise.

ALABAMA is the last stop on the great Appalachian mountain system that began its long march in Quebec. Here along the lines where the ridges and valleys flatten out, a wide swath of heavy, fertile soil cuts across the central part of the state. Known as "the Black Belt," this region was for a long time the basis of a cotton economy and a planter aristocracy; today it is largely devoted to cattle raising and poultry farming. The regions to the north and south of the Black Belt present very different faces. The hilly north has rich deposits of coal and iron ore, which led to the founding of Birmingham in 1871 and a steel-industry boom

Top to bottom: *Last in the string of Florida Keys, Key West is as far south as you can go in the continental United States. Inhabitants call themselves "Conchs" and the convoluted shell is their emblem. This gracious residence with fountain is called Southernmost House. Fort Jefferson, built in the 1800s, occupies one of the late Dry Tortugas, an island group 60 miles from Key West.*

Ernest Hemingway House in Key West, where the novelist worked in the 1930s, is now a popular museum. Below: *Entrance to the John and Mabel Ringling Museum of Art, Sarasota, a treasure house of European painting and sculpture displayed in cloister-like galleries and formal garden.*

Opposite: *Doge's Palace in Venice was model for Ca' d'Zan ("John's house"), built by circus impresario John Ringling for his wife in 1924-26. Public may tour the 32-room mansion in Sarasota.* This page: *It takes about two hours to tour Sunken Gardens, a lush botanical park on Tampa Bay in St. Petersburg. Until it upped anchor and made for Miami, the Bounty, replica made for the film* Mutiny on the Bounty, *was a favorite tourist attraction in St. Petersburg.*

that lasted until the Great Depression. South of the Black Belt the land is rolling, red, and piney until it reaches the flat coastal plain.

The delta of the Mobile River, with its colorful, cosmopolitan city of Mobile, makes up the southernmost part of the state, on the Gulf of Mexico. Known since its French beginnings as a pleasure-loving city, Mobile beguiles visitors with its beautiful gardens and houses bedecked with lacy ironwork.

MISSISSIPPI is chiefly rural, and although there are many industries and a diversified agriculture, cotton is as much an economic mainstay today as it was in the days of the great plantations. Natchez and Vicksburg on the Mississippi River are especially rich in pre-Civil War houses, and the town of Holly Springs in the north has been called "an antebellum jewel."

Top to bottom: *Court Square Fountain, by sculptor Frederick MacMonnies, is a cherished 1885 landmark in Alabama's capital city, Montgomery. Birmingham-Jefferson Civic Center, with special facilities for conventions, concerts, theater, and sports, opened in 1970; at center here is the Concert Hall. Mobile, on the Gulf Coast of Alabama, is one of the nation's important ports.*

Above: *A display of rockets greets visitors to the Alabama Space and Rocket Center in the fast-growing city of Huntsville.* Below: *Saved from the scrap heap, the USS* Alabama *is open for tours at its own Battleship Park in Mobile.*

This page: *Though the exterior of Longwood promises magnificence, the interior walls were never finished, work being abandoned in 1861. It is the largest octagonal house in the United States and one of many splendid houses in Natchez. Spanish moss shadows this section of the Old Natchez Trace, a footpath that traversed the country between Natchez and Nashville. Now the two-lane Natchez Trace Parkway, a national park, parallels the historic route.*

Right: *This small temple is one of many memorials at the Vicksburg National Military Park, site of Grant's siege and capture of the Mississippi port town.* Below: *The gunboat* Cairo, *a Union ironclad sunk in the attack on Vicksburg, has been raised and placed on display at the Military Park.*

Students of the Civil War will be fascinated by the many battle sites. Grant's siege and capture of Vicksburg is reconstructed at the Vicksburg National Military Park. Crucial battles raged over rail lines in the northeast and are commemorated at the Brice Cross Roads and Tupelo National Battlefield sites.

One of the state's most famous residents was the Nobel Prize-winner novelist William Faulkner, who lived and worked for much of his life in Oxford. He and other writers such as Eudora Welty, Shelby Foote, and Walker Percy constitute a remarkable literary tradition, sprung from the culture of this deepest of the Deep South states.

Panorama of New Orleans at dusk.

Top to bottom: *The best-known feature of the modern city is the Superdome, annual site of football's climactic Superbowl Game. The New Orleans skyline reflects the city's status as a major banking center and one of the busiest ports in the world.*

LOUISIANA was part of the land that the United States purchased from France in 1803 for $15 million. At that time the people of New Orleans and the surrounding region were a cultural mix that included, besides Native Americans, people from France, Spain, Acadia (French Nova Scotia), Germany, Italy, and Africa. Then, as now, New Orleans was unique.

The city should be on every traveler's itinerary. Its heart is the Vieux Carré, where there are spacious plazas, narrow streets, and houses with ornamental ironwork. Jazz was born in New Orleans and the city keeps the tradition alive in many music clubs, especially in tiny Preservation Hall, the place to hear New Orleans jazz in its purest form.

To know Louisiana one needs to break out of the orbit of New Orleans. To the southwest is "Cajun country," a place of sluggish bayous and lively people; Lafayette, the region's unofficial capital, has many structures from its early settlement days. Along the routes north toward Baton Rouge, the state capital, lie many plantation houses that are open to the public. (Note that in Louisiana, travel is between "parishes," not "counties.")

Flower lovers will delight in the state's many gardens, such as the 118-acre American Rose Center near Shreveport.

Like many subjects, the South is far greater than the sum of its parts. While the image of it created by *Gone With The Wind* will live forever in our hearts, it too is only part of the greater whole: a region filled with historic treasure and vital cultural heritage, and with a firm grasp on the future.

Opposite: *Many buildings in the French Quarter, or Vieux Carré, are adorned with fanciful ironwork. This page: Mardi Gras (literally "fat Tuesday") is the day citizens of "The Big Easy" put on costumes and greasepaint and join in a city-wide celebration. The vibrant art of Dixieland jazz lives on behind the unassuming façade of Preservation Hall, where leading musicians play nightly to a packed house. If you can't get in, you can listen at the windows.*

St. Louis Cathedral overlooks Jackson Square, main ceremonial plaza of the French Quarter. Notable for its three spires, the church has been raised to the status of a minor basilica. **Opposite:** *Another day ends in the quiet bayou country along the Amite River in Livingston Parish.*

Index of Photography

All photographs courtesy of The Image Bank,
except where indicated*